THE FALSE MASTERS OF ECKANKAR

JOE SYKES

Freedom from Cult Abuse Inc.

THE FALSE MASTERS OF ECKANKAR

THE FALSE MASTERS OF ECKANKAR

THE FALSE MASTERS OF ECKANKAR

INTRODUCTION

The False Masters of Eckankar explains what the Eckankar organisation *really* is. Cutting through the marketeering, jargon and buzz words, through the pseudo-Hindu guru cult pretensions, through the childishly bizarre claims, this is a fresh and unsparing look at how this Californian group actually works and what happens in membership.

The author is a former member, of 14 years' vintage, so this is an insider's view. The author shares insights and knowledge learned in over 40 years of religious and spiritual experience, including in his adopted Christian faith, which expose this damaging cult to a new, harsh light.

But I hear you say, as a 6th initiate: *Oh, why would I need to read that? I'm happy doing my spiritual exercises once or twice a week, and sitting in the audience minding my own business once in a while at a seminar.*

Easy. The reason you would need to read this book, despite your fanciful belief you enjoy an elevated status, is because, with the greatest of respect, you have no idea what you've gotten yourself into.

The False Masters of Eckankar is written for you.

July 2020

THE FALSE MASTERS OF ECKANKAR

Contents

1

The Invented Order of the Vairagi

1.1 The line of Eck Masters

The founder of the Eckankar cult in California in 1965, Paul Twitchell, was a pupil of the Hindu guru system.

That system is simple. A learned religious man sets himself up to educate others in his knowledge. He is the guru; they are his pupils.

Twitchell's gurus included Swami Premananda and Kirpal Singh.[1] Both of these gurus had their gurus, who had their gurus, and so on back in time. They were relaxed about their pupils; essentially, pupils were free to stay or go.

Twitchell was too canny, and far too much the egotist to be satisfied with that system. Having decided he was fit to be a guru, he wanted much more control over his pupils. He therefore wrote in his early books describing Eckankar that it descended from an ancient line of gurus that he called Masters.

Twitchell's line was a far more rigorous structure than a mere line of gurus. It borrowed the language of the United States

---

[1] The nature of Twitchell's relationship with these gurus is analysed in *The Truth About Eckankar*.

Presidents, in 1965 said to be an unbroken line of 35 Presidents. Twitchell decided on the much more impressive number of 971.

This he called the Order of Vairagi. Into this Order Twitchell dragged a litany of famous names. One was the Italian Catholic saint, St Francis of Assissi, who as every child knows talked to the animals. Two other real life teachers were Rumi, the Sufi poet, and Lao Tse, the Chinese poet, who Twitchell slightly renamed Lao Tsi.

Some of these 'Masters' had bizarrely unlikely names. Like Rebazar Tarzs, who Twitchell named as his personal guru. Research into Twitchell's books shows he substituted the name of Tarzs for his principal real-life guru, Swami Premananda, in his book *The Tiger's Fang*.[2]

Tarzs was made up. Twitchell switched his name in, taking out the Swami's, to avoid claims that Twitchell's Eckankar was derivative (as it was) of the books of the Swami and Kirpal Singh (as it was).

Twitchell did not stop there. He made Rebazar Tarzs centre stage in his personal universe as time went on. Tarzs' His commanding personality was drawn closely from the overbearing, egotistical personality of Swami Premananda.

This particular fabrication is important, as Twitchell elevated Tarzs to the title of 'Torchbearer of Eck', holding the flame of spirituality for the world. Oops. No torchbearer, folks.

Other unlikely names included Gopal Das. A gentleman with a name of that type can only have been born in India. It is an extremely common Indian name.

Twitchell reimagined Mr Das as a tall, Nordic blond man. In a further twist, he placed his Mastership in ancient Egypt. So

---

[2] See books by David Lane.

Twitchell had a common Indian name for a Nordic blond who lived in Egypt. This must have been a bad night at the typewriter.

1.2 Tibet and the black magicians in Eckankar

One interesting facet of the list of 971 Masters was that Twitchell could barely think of 20 real life or fabricated people. Another was the confusion of Tibetan magicians with Indian gurus.

Twitchell borrowed his theology of gurus, Shabda Yoga, out of body travel and pupillage from his own gurus.

But the strong characters in his imagined line are not, in fact, Hindu.

They are *Tibetan*.

The only man with a Hindu name was Gopal Das, and he was recast as Egyptian by way of Norway.

Oh, you ask, why does that matter?

Well, we'll see.

1.2 Tibet and black magicians in Eckankar

The imagined characters of Rebazar Tarzs, Yaubl Sacabi, respectively a Tibetan monk wearing a maroon robe who has the role of the principal guru in the world, and the bald head of an underground Tibetan monastery, have nothing to do with Hindu guru systems.

A related and wildly imagined fact was that Mastership in Eckankar passes on the night of the 21st October at midnight in the fabled valley of Tirmir, a deserted place in Tibet. This is a world away from instructive daylight sessions at a guru's ashram.

What kind of religious practitioner, it is fair to ask, meets at midnight?

It is a fair assumption that Twitchell had read into Tibetan books of spells and black magic and had decided, as a shrewd marketeer, to use their force to add punch to his fabricated cosmology.

In this, Twitchell was continuing the influence of the Swami, who, outwardly a yogic teacher, was at the same time an advanced practitioner of black magic. His reading into black magic – the use of occult power for personal gain - would have included books of Tibetan spells and their many ancient works about magic and black magic.

None of this has anything to do with Hindu guru systems and the gentle acquisition of religious knowledge.

The key is Twitchell's placement of the real life Tibetan saint Milarepa as the head of the Vairagi Order. Milarepa is famous in Tibet as an extremely powerful black magician.[3]

Twitchell, therefore, used the theology he picked up from the Swami and Kirpal Singh (who he renamed Sudar Singh in his books), but for punch he relied on real life and invented Tibetan magicians and monasteries.

---

[33] *The Life and Songs of Milarepa*, Tsangnyon Heruka. See also below.

THE FALSE MASTERS OF ECKANKAR

A way to understand the resultant Eckankar theology is not to look at its surface and wonder about what is made up, what is borrowed, but to peer through the surface, turn back and look at it from behind.

In this way, you see more easily the patchwork nature of the composition. Bits and pieces from various religious and magic systems, together with pure fabricated elements, sit uneasily together.

The reason the composition works at all, for a period of time until its spell fades, is the fact that a member of Eckankar is under the influence of the leader, who is a powerful black magician.

That is, a skilled practitioner of occult forces who manipulates them for personal benefit, as opposed to the work of the white magicians, who act always for the good of the Earth and its inhabitants.

Welcome to Eckankar: the New Age 60s Californian out of body travel group, mixed in with Hindu Shabda Yoga theology, these elements being used as an ingenious *cover* for a control-obsessed group run by ruthless, exploitative, unforgiving practitioners of black magic techniques.

Oh My God! I hear you say. *What have I got into here?*

You got yourself into a Tibetan black magic group.

The Tibetan god of hell

1.3 Living eck masters or black magicians?

Lest this be shocking news to any initiate, please remember the recent published history of the cult's leadership. Both Twitchell's successor Darwin Gross and the current leader Harold Klemp, *accused each other* of using black magic to harm the other.

In autumn 1981 Gross was exhausted, overweight and unwell after ten years as leader. The Board of Trustees of Eckankar removed him as leader and substituted the unknown initiate Harold Klemp as a compromise candidate for the new 'Master.' Gross was given a lifetime role and payment to keep him quiet.

However, by 1983, amid stories of Gross using initiates' wives for sex, and stealing millions of dollars from the organisation's bank accounts, leading to litigation against Gross in the courts in Portland, Oregon, the deal broke up.

Gross alleged Klemp was employing *'the dark arts'* and *'necromancy'* to attack him.

Klemp came back with an article titled *'Methods of the Black Magician'*, darkly accusing Gross of using black magic to control members' minds.[4]

The accusations were puerile and pointless, as both men were using black magic techniques against the other in their grab for members.

---

[4] In 1983 Gross was dismissed, and the cult split. Gross started his own cult called ATOM in Portland, with himself as Master. It was followed by those who adhered to him rather than to Klemp.

1.4 Thought control in Eckankar

Central to Eckankar practice and culture is thought control. Thought control, the introduction of a thought into a target member's mind, its promotion with emotional feelings and sensations, the acceptance of the thought, and the introduction of further thoughts that build control, is basic to the Eckankar leadership.

Thought control works just like a hacker's trojan programme. It finds a way in, and gradually builds control. At a certain point, the member loses control over his own mind, and the leader has control.

1.5 How to break thought control

It should be mentioned that this passing of control to the Eck Master is entirely a matter of belief. If the member recognises what has happened, no matter how many years have passed since it started, and ceases to believe in the rightness of the original thought, the thought control structure built into his mind immediately loses power.

It can then be fully identified, broken off, and removed from the mind by the individual member. Eckankar's control over you is entirely dependent on your belief.

1.6 The desire for power and control

One may add here that the key to your belief in Eckankar's theology and practice is the (mistaken) desire for power. The Eckankar membership is frankly riddled with power-mad people, and by lust and perceived need for power consciously or unconsciously living in the minds of members.

Singing *Hu* all day or getting nine initiations will not change a thing. Most members never change at all. What is required to bring about real personal change in the Eckankar member is to recognise the nature of the thought structure built into their minds, detach themselves from it, and begin the task of breaking every thought in it off their mind and its memories.

Why is that? Because the very thoughts in the mental structure you have accepted are themselves composed as a result of the lust for power and control. Twitchell, like the Swami, were men who wanted power to dominate others.

All Twitchell's thoughts, properly analysed, are *thoughts of power*. Power in the concepts of the Sugmad, Eck, Mahanta, Fifth Plane, 14th Plane, soul travel. Power in the requirement for the member's absolute submission to the leader. Power conferred on the member by the series of initiations (as in Freemasonry).

And who is it that is focused on thoughts of power? It is the black magician. Twitchell was a highly experienced magician, boasting of his ability to control the weather, just like Milarepa (who attached his enemies with bad weather). Gross and Klemp are squabbling, power-crazy children compared to Twitchell.

1.7 Twitchell's control over Eckankar

The uncomfortable truth, explored further on in this book, is that the real leader of the cult remains Paul Twitchell.

Twitchell is Eckankar's dark lord, but a depressive, miserable version, one who resides in darkness and attacks with phenomenal violence and viciousness when annoyed or when desirous of exercising power over a target.

Like the fictional Voldemort, Twitchell has placed, and depends on, a great many horcruxes on Earth.

Twitchell's very ability to control the group depends on his ability to keep those horcruxes in place.

His key horcruxes are:

(1)   the Eckankar international office,

(2)   the current 'Master', who he controls absolutely,

(3)   the continuing earthy life of those he initiated himself,

(4)   the goodwill and above all good memories of him in the older initiates,

(5)   the continuing sale of his books and photographs.

Like Voldemort, Twitchell lives in and by your memories.

Every time a member breaks off the belief in Twitchell, his self described mastership and his false cosmology, a horcrux dies and Twitchell is weakened.

Right now, Klemp's failure to build the cult after the loss of Gross, who made Eckankar as a growing force, and Klemp's retreat from the membership, has led to the cult failing. Twitchell is losing horcruxes all the time. This is an inevitable process. However, as an experienced magician, bound to his techniques of power and control, Twitchell will not relinquish a single horcrux without a battle.

This was the meaning of Klemp's reference in his public talk printed in *How to find God*, about the fate of the female Eckist who left and became a Lutheran.

This Eckist received harassing visits in her dreams from Klemp and others, criticising her for being fat, etc.

She found her marriage fell apart, and she lost her job. She read the tea leaves, decided to play safe and not incur any more disaster, and ran back to the cult.

In a deceptively light and humorous way, Klemp was threatening destruction of the personal life to any member who dared to leave.

This was no different to Twitchell threatening doom to leavers, stating they would be placed 'in astral hells.'

The task of dismantling the false Eckankar thought structure inside your mind, and the battle to stop you from 'the Eck', ie the leadership, will be greatly assisted by a humble and honest submission to God.

Secondly, by seeking out a Christian born-again church that has a reputation for the Living Spirit, and being born again there in God.

Where does this point lead?

As a member, you are caught in the spider's web of the magician, cocooned around and around with the silk of incantation and obedience.

Every time you sing Hu and imagine Klemp in the 3rd Eye, you pitch yourself deeper into his control, and the power that controls him.

This is simple, plain and obvious. Yet hard to see, and very hard to fight.

You may find the Eckankar discourses deadly dull and endlessly repetitive, the books unconscionably tedious.[5]

They are.

But the *reason* you keep reading, and keep doing the vacuous spiritual exercises, is that you are under a spell, caught within the influence of a dominating, draining, dumbing-down magical power.

1.8 The Rod of Power

The specific power in Eckankar was introduced by Twitchell, and has been maintained by his successors. They call it *The Rod of Power*.

The grandiose title of Mahanta, living eck master, describes in the cult's theology/mythology the man who accepts the power within himself, as intermediary between the Silent Ones and the material world.

This is the reason advanced by the cult for justifying belief in 'the living master.' The world, they say, needs a *living* master to hold the Rod of Power.

But is this reason true in any sense, including spiritually?

Look at the facts. Many ordinary Christians testify that they experience, and in some cases see clearly, Jesus Christ, in the spiritual form of the man who lived in ancient Israel, and whose life is celebrated in the New Testament.

Jesus helps countless people, particularly the weak, vulnerable, broken. Yet he is based in the heavens.

---

[5] The *Shariyat ki Sugmad*, anyone? Twitchell's attempt to write scripture fails miserably as it subjects the reader to mind-numbing boredom with repetition of similar phrases.

In Islam, Jesus is celebrated as a prophet, not the Christ. Yet Islam accepts that, at the end of the world, it is Jesus who returns to pass judgment. That is precisely what is written in Revelation, the last book of the New Testament.

Christianity and Islam happen to be the two most followed religions in the world. Is it truly tenable to argue their entire memberships are the object of mass deception?

And if so, practiced by *who*? Who is it that conjures up the image of Jesus to visit those suffering smashed, horrific lives?

Reality check 1, folks:

Jesus appears to the millions because he is the expression in form of the Holy Spirit of God, who commands from the highest heaven.

Reality check 2:

Paul Twitchell never travelled to the 14th Plane (as he calls it), because, in the *Tiger's Fang*, his single testimony of spiritual travel to God, he copied the descriptions of the highest planes from JP Johnson's *The Path of the Masters*.

Have you noticed that, in the *Tiger's Fang*, as he gets into the highest planes, Twitchell has virtually nothing to say?

Because Twitchell only *read* about the high planes of God described by Johnson, and known to the Sant Mat and Radhasoami Hindu spiritual groups. Therefore *to describe his 14 planes he had to resort to copying another writer*.

Have you also noticed that the main incident in that portion of Twitchell's *Tiger's Fang* is his body being savaged by a cruel, torturing being? And that that is wholly inconsistent with the otherworldly peace he attributes to those planes?

The answer is simple. The characteristics of this torturing being are *precisely* those he separately attributes to Kal/Jot Niranjan, his fabled astral plane ruler (i.e., Satan)? To add something to JP Johnson's descriptions, Twitchell adds in a low, emotional, quasi-physical experience.

What added value, by the way, does the living Eck leader provide members? Klemp takes an Eckist out of the body into a sensory experience. So what? Where is the spiritual change?

The problem with the current Eckankar membership is lack of spiritual change. They are stuck, *'frozen in time'* to use a phrase Klemp borrowed from a letter written him by a former English member, Krisha Murthi. Year after year, initiation after initiation, and – what happened? Zilch.

The writer of this book was a member for 14 years. On leaving, and coming back to life, he discovered he was 14 years older, but actually no different in emotional terms.

Even his body had not changed that much. He calls those years *the lost years*. Nothing changed spiritually.

Zilch.

Since leaving, and becoming a Christian reborn in the Holy Spirit, the writer has experienced incredible spiritual change. Incredible addition of spiritual gifts. Incredible increase and refinement of existing gifts. Spiritual change? Fantastic.

The writer of this book has described how Klemp and others have subjected him to repeated psychic, violent occult attack. Out of jealousy and fury that the writer could find living spirituality in Christianity. Of course they're furious. They're liars and they're crooks sitting on piles of tame members' cash. They've been caught out.

The writer, like tens of thousands of Christians, has experienced the living reality of the Holy Spirit directly within him. And why is that? Not because he read bizarre books stuffed with fabrication and worked on Hindu guru out of body travel. Not a bit of it.

The key to true spiritual change, and the birth of the Holy Spirit within, is to get on your knees before God and humbly beg His forgiveness for your lifelong self-importance and lack of faith.

And accept Jesus as your loving, living spiritual master in an act of pure faith.

Then the Holy Spirit of God can come in.

There is, therefore, no *spiritual* need for a living master. The actual purpose of the living eck master in Eckankar originates in the darkest occult practices.

His function is to act as a facilitator for the occult purpose of transmitting this demonic and ferocious, and – may we say – utterly violent power to the Earth, so it can be used to exercise power here more easily.

Klemp justified building the cult's temple in Chanhassen, Minnesota, as meeting the need for 'a seat of power', just as the Catholic Church has St Peter's in Rome.

Truly, it is a power, and a formidable one; and one very difficult to escape. It is extremely conscious of your every movement, and watches you day and night like a cruel cat watches an innocent baby mouse that has wandered into its grasp in search of food. The little bit of cheese this cat places in front of the mouse, which the mouse foolishly accepts, is poisoned with delusion.

However, the Eckankar power is vastly inferior to the true spiritual power of the Holy Spirit known to a Christian humbled and born again in the Spirit, which can displace and dissipate the magic power in Eckankar in a fraction of a second.

When the Holy Spirit is truly present, the power of Eckankar, held and wielded by its 'Masters', instantly leaves in fear and in recognition of the overwhelming superiority of the Holy Spirit.

1.9 The Nine Silent Ones

Which brings us, neatly enough, to the Nine Silent Ones. These beings are described in Twitchell's *The Far Country*. Under his successors, Gross and Klemp, the Nine Silent Ones were talked about much more, albeit in hushed tones.

Initiates have implicitly accepted what Twitchell wanted them to accept: that *mere knowledge* of the Nine Silent Ones conferred an unspeakable level of privilege and spiritual importance.

In the Far Country the Nine Silent Ones are described by the fabricated teacher, Rebazar Tarzs, talking in his hut in Tibet, as the highest beings in creation, serving directly the highest god, the Sugmad, and taking instructions from him for the management of living beings.

Twitchell's teacher claims these beings are 'the Mahavakyis, the Silent Travelers and so mighty are these great ones that you seldom can confront them.'

Let's stop here for a second. The Mahavakyis – a Hindu word –don't exist in Hinduism. Twitchell liked the word and adapted it from the Hindu theological term *Mahavakya*.

The Mahavakyas are the four main sayings of the Upanishads, a key text in Advaita Vedanta. The Mahavakyas are:

(1)   Brahman is Prajñāna;
(2)   This Self) is Brahman;
(3)   Thou art that;
(4)   I am Brahman (Divine).

Tarzs (i.e., Twitchell) calls the Mahavikyas the 'silent ones.'

Who are the Nine Silent Ones, or the Council of the Nine, however?

Leaving aside Twitchell's wildly fanciful invention, designed to make the initiate feel part of an impossibly superior spiritual universe, and therefore unable to imagine leaving the group, is there any truth to these beings?

The answer is: no, and yes. No, because Twitchell was lying again. Yes, because there is a group of powerful spirits guiding aspects of Earth life, but they are quite different from his amateur cartoon.

During the Gross period, they were regarded as incredibly powerful, able to break the universe in a split second, and therefore not to be approached.

An example of that quality of uncaring violence appears in Phil Morimitsu's book *In the Company of Eck Masters*. There is a reference to a disruption occurring nearby, which Twitchell, appearing now as a departed spirit to Morimitsu, describes as *'silent one passing.'*

Another insight. An English initiate called Graham Forsyth fell out with the Eckankar International Office and Harold Klemp in 2001 when Eckist friends wrote to a 7th Initiate, Ford Johnson, claiming to be a higher initiate than Klemp, and personally under the guidance of the Nine Silent Ones.

Mr Forsyth's story was that, while the Eckankar Master is an initiate of the 14th Plane, he personally was an initiate of the 16th Plane. He told friends that the Nine Silent Ones had appeared around him, friendly and smiling, and generally very happy with him.

Mr Forsyth believed he was under the personal training of the Nine Silent Ones.

Klemp's response was to put Ford Johnson on a six month warning, with the punishment of having to read the unreadably tedious Shariyat Ki Sugmad Book I, and for further measure, the somewhat undisciplined and hollow Shariyat ki Sugmad Book II.

As for poor Mr Forsyth, he was demoted to the 1st Initiation. Klemp, a control freak, was quick to control what he saw as emerging challengers to this title.[6]

The reality is that the supposedly silent spirits seen by members are demonic spirits of the lower heavens, with an earthly base in Tibet. The presence of the Holy Spirit is too strong on Earth for these spirits to manifest. So they appear occasionally to those who are individually receptive to them.

The number nine was Twitchell's marketeering idea. He apparently thought the number, expressing a perfect expression of the primal number three by self-multiplication (i.e., three x three), resonated with simplicity and power. It was a theatrical addition to an ugly reality.

Twitchell's head of the Vairagi, Milarepa, is famous in Tibetan occult history for mastering demonic spirits. Born Mila Thopaga Josay, and living 83 years during the Western

---

[6] Another bizarre claim was by Michael Owens, who wrote a book called *Shariyat ki Sugmad IV*, and claimed to have been initiated as the 974th Master, with the spiritual name Dan Rin. This was of course a transparent corruption of Darwin Gross' own purported spiritual name, Dap Ren.

medieval era, approximately AD 1052 – 1135, Milarepa mastered demonic spirits when placed in his cave by his teacher Marpa.

Milarepa tried to control the spirits with ritual incantation, and failed badly. He succeeded only when he realised they were a manifestation of his own mind. He asserted his belief in his positive occult accomplishments and rushed them, causing them to be terrified. Immediately, they resolved into one spirit, and then disappeared.[7]

After that, no demonic spirit could touch him.

Here's a picture of Milarepa, widely known during his life as a ferocious magician and as a mad monk...

---

[7] http://buddhism.lib.ntu.edu.tw/FULLTEXT/JR-EPT/simm.htm

You can see the madness in the man. He lived on nettle soup, and that turned his skin green.

Let's now go back to the origin of the 'nine silent ones.'

Twitchell, who read fast and understood little, was instinctively attracted to the Dhamapalas, a group of eight angry spirits who control the Tibetan hell.[8]

The highest of the Dhamapalas is Yama. Yama, also known in Tibetan occult theology as the King of Hell, has the function of judging the dead and ruling purgatorial hells known as the Narakas.

Remember in *Child in the Wilderness*, rewritten as *Modern Prophet*, Klemp attempts to commit suicide in Milwaukee in the belief he must climb the Mountain of Yama? There Klemp describes Yama as death.

Yama, in fact, is pictured in Tibet as a demon. Here is a picture:

---

[8] Twitchell evened out the eight Dhamapalas into nine silent ones

THE FALSE MASTERS OF ECKANKAR

In Tibet, Yama is regarded as the head of the Dharmapalas, eight demons who guard their followers. Twitchell renamed the eight demons as nine silent ones.

One of these is Palden Lhamo, the only female Dharmapala. She was renamed Kata Daki by Twitchell and given a new role of an 'eck master' guiding Eckankar members.

Twitchell/Klemp's adoption of the demon Yama as a concept is an incomplete digestion of a significant Tibetan occult belief. Yama is not merely death – i.e., for Klemp, the fear of death – but the judge of the spiritually fallen.

Klemp confused physical death (his fear) with spiritual death (his reality). Klemp's account reflects immature understanding of the spiritual meaning of death, which is the fall from God.

What is more significant is Klemp's unthinking adoption of the concept of the Mountain of Yama from his teacher, Twitchell. The key to it is Twitchell's contemptuous leading of his pupil into a false belief, just as the Tibetan teacher Marpa led Milarepa into false belief in the cave.

A second point to be drawn from this incident is the introduction of the hellish spirit Yama into the centre of Eckankar theology through Klemp's misconceived main autobiographical books.

Dead centre in the psychic character of Harold Klemp, and the psychic character of Eckankar, right now, is the ruling spirit of the Tibetan hell.

The character of the 'Nine Silent Ones', is generally abrupt and extremely violent. That is precisely the character of the Tibetan Dhamapalas. They are also determined and persistent. In 1965 they used Twitchell to introduce the violent, possessive dark power that is at the centre of Eckankar.

Twitchell came to their attention while a disciple of Swami Premananda in the 1950s. The Swami was a high level Freemason who had been initiated at the 33rd degree of the Scottish Rite into the service of the powerful demonic spirit popularly known as Lucifer.

The Silent Ones later used Gross to try, and Klemp to succeed, in obtaining an earthly location for this power. Klemp manage it in construction of the Chanhassen 'temple'. This place gives the Silent Ones a physical location on Earth more permanent for their power than that of the human Master.

Carol Geraci sued Eckankar after working in the so-called 'temple.' She said that at night it was a weird, violent place, which often scared her, and troubled her sleep.

Hardly surprising when you consider the 'eck temple' is a landing ground for Tibetan demons.

Have you noticed that while the theology of Eckankar is Hindu, the people associations are principally Tibetan? Why is it that Twitchell located the initiation of the living eck master in the Valley of Tirmir... in Tibet?[9] Where is the hut of the fabricated person Rebazar Tarza? Tibet. Where is the monastery controlled by the monk Twitchell called Yaubl Sacabi? Tibet. Who is the head of the Vairagi Order? Milarepa, the Tibetan magician. Tibet and Tibetans are at the *centre* of the cult.

The Nine Silent Ones are at the centre of Eckankar. These Dhamapalas are the key to the real explanation for its creation and existence.

---

[9] Where do 'eck masters' throw rocks at each other? A place where are there rocks... like a mountain, of which Tibet has many.

THE FALSE MASTERS OF ECKANKAR

Because Eckankar is no Hindu guru cult, boys and girls. The exterior clothing of Shabda Yoga theology and practice is mere cover for a Tibetan black magic cult, rooted in power and control, and used and controlled by these powerful demonic spirits.

The presence of the Eckankar cult on Earth is, consequently, a potential threat to every living being.

Thankfully, the cult is poorly subscribed, an uninspiring and now failing transplant from Tibet.

The cult is principally as an example of the psychic entrapment and spiritual deathliness and suffering that attends those who seek power instead of God in a cult promising everything and giving back an empty, hypnotised, suffering existence.

2

Sugmad

2.1   What is Sugmad?

Let's start with the name. The name for God in Eckankar, *Sugmad*, is *a made up name.*   In the book Twitchell copied most, JP Johnson's *The Path of the Masters*, using chunks of it for *The Tiger's Fang* and other books, there is no reference to a Sugmad.

Nor is there any reference to Sugmad in any religion on Earth.

Here is JP Johnson listing names for God to be found in the Hindu Radhasoami and Sant Mat Hindu traditions (at pages 221 - 222):

'In the literature of the Saints, God is expressed by many words, such as Swami, Ekankar, Nirankar, Radhaswami, Akal, Nirala, Anami, Agam, Alakh, Sat Purush, Prabhu, Prabhswami, Hari Ray, Akshar, Parameshwar, Akshar Purush, etc.

'All of these words have been coined in an effort to convey to human intelligence some idea of what the Saints think of God, or Lord God, the highest power. Ekankar means the "One oneness," the body of oneness. Nirankar means without body or form. Soami or Swami means the all-pervading Lord. Radha Swami – Radha (soul) and Swami (Lord) – the Lord of the soul – Radha, when reversed, becomes dhara or current. As soul has to revert to its source, so its dhara, when reversed, when its current is turned toward God, becomes Radha. ... The whole universe is considered as one, the true Ekankar.'

Twitchell, a keen marketeer with a sense of what would sell to the (then) relatively innocent and impressionable American public, made up the name Sugmad to distinguish it from the Hindu names. He wanted a name that stood apart. So he made it up.

The fact of this invention is not a joke. Twitchell was not the mischievous, eccentric joker Klemp would have Eckists believe.

Twitchell was a hustler and a salesman who was on the make to make money. He had a depressive personality that without notice could turn violent and physically violent.

Here Twitchell was playing with the holiest concepts in Hindu religion. The names of God that JP Johnson lists are spiritual facts, not mere collections of syllables. The names have a sound that evokes a reality.

For Twitchell, that was bunkum. He cheerfully make up a name purely to be different and not be accused of being like other groups. Indeed, that is the essential project of Eckankar in the marketplace: to look and sound different, so as to convince recruits it was different.

Of course, the Eckankar group was not different at all. It was entirely derivative of other men's books. Theologically, it was a mere collection of concepts copied (i.e. stolen) from JP Johnson, Kirpal Singh, and the Radhasoami and Sant Mat traditions.

Eckankar is a group founded on copyright theft. It continues to be partly financed on copyright theft, as it is not declaring copyright usage nor paying copyright payments to the authors Twitchell stole from.

You will also see in the excerpt above that Twitchell pinched the spelling of Ekankar and westernised it as Eckankar. It derives from the Sikh symbol *Ik Onkar*. The symbol is drawn thus:

This symbol means refers to the supreme reality of God in Sikhism. It means 'God is One.'

The Sikh saint Guru Nanak referred to the original God as 'Oankar.'

Twitchell copied and simplified the word and symbol, into Eckankar and a glorified capital E. The rounded E is discernible inside the symbol above.

Thus high spiritual reality and the fusion of idea and sound in the Ik Onkar symbol, were marketed and dumbed down into the odd name 'eckankar' and the familiar-but-different use of a rounded E symbol.

2.2 Sugmad vs God

Ok then: if Sugmad is a fabrication, something spun out of Twitchell's head, does that mean there is no god in Eckankar?

Yes and no. Yes, it means there is no god in Eckankar. Eckankar's claim to be a religion is a fraud.

No, there are *gods* in Eckankar. They just happen to be Tibetan gods. Or rather, ferocious demonic spirits. See above, section 1.9.

Translated into Western religious concepts, the gods in Eckankar are the servants of Lucifer, the fallen Archangel, the most senior hellish demon.

The hard reality for the membership is that the real name of Eckankar's god is not Sugmad, but Lucifer. The archangel of light, fallen into magic tricks, is quite clearly the god Twitchell worshipped and followed. *The Tiger's Fang* and its journey to the high heavens simply ripped off JP Johnson. Its conception is the Radhasoami version of a 1960s acid trip. Twitchell's actual life experience was of the hustle, of conflict with everyone, of his own violent nature.

The Swami was the person through whom the powerful demonic spirit Lucifer drew in Twitchell and still controls that little man.

The evidence for this fact - to some perhaps a startling assertion - is overwhelming:

(1)   There is an appalling lack of love, compassion in the Eckankar leadership. Klemp talks about God's love, but doesn't show any. Instead, he's a self-centred recluse.

(2)   Initiates in trouble are left to suffer. Carol Geraci's response to the writer complaining of psychic attack by the particularly vicious leader Harold Klemp was 'You should get a doctor.' This particular initiate epitomises the egoism in Eckankar leaders. She seeks out young male initiates for sex (as witnessed by the writer at seminars) to satisfy herself, yet when a fellow initiate is in trouble, she hasn't the time. That is Klemp's Eckankar all over — selfish and rotten to the core.

(3)   Eckankar displays a key operating principle of the occult: substitution. That means it does not offer the reality – such as Yah Weh in Christianity – but a plausible substitute for it. Substitution is the basis of Lucifer's existence. Wanting to substitute himself for God, he was demoted. So to salve his status, Lucifer claims Godlike power. However, he has only substitution to offer. Instead of humility he offers knowledge and pride.

(4)   Eckankar, similarly, does not offer humility before God, but the distractions of astral travel and all of 14 borrowed 'planes'.

2.3 Sugmad and the living eck master

A key claim to spiritual superiority in the cult is that Sugmad appoints the living eck master.

So, Harold Klemp was appointed not just by God, but by the highest god, Sugmad? Seriously?

Excuse us, this is nonsense.

Eckankar records contradict this fabrication. Let's start with Twitchell. Where is the evidence the highest god appointed him to anything? Twitchell *appointed himself.* Contrary to the claim of an unbroken line of almost 1, 000 'masters', he had no predecessor whatsoever.

Next, Darwin Gross. Gross was not appointed by his purported predecessor, Twitchell. Gross was appointed in October 1971 by Twitchell's widow Gail Twitchell. T(2) Sugmad appoints the living eck master

Eckankar records contradict this fabrication. Twitchell appointed himself, there being no predecessor. Darwin Gross was appointed in October 1971 by Twitchell's widow Gail Twitchell, following her husband's unexpected death in Cincinnati in September 1971. Harold Klemp was appointed by the Eckankar Board of Trustees, headed by Peter Skelskey in 1981 after the Board deposed Darwin Gross. So much for the role of the imaginary Sugmad.

As a footnote, despite Twitchell's claims of an endless line of Eckankar Masters, Klemp has stated there will be no successor. The line ends with him. Sugmad has apparently retired.

More seriously, the test of a man's spirituality is of course his actual conduct. By their fruit shall ye know them. Twitchell was a pathological liar, driven by the desire to obtain money, not to foster religious education.

Gross was terminated by the Board of Trustees in 1981 while sleeping with senior initiates' wives, then sued in the courts in Portland, Oregon in 1983 – 1987 for the return of $2.5m he allegedly stole from the cult's accounts.

Klemp added a quasi-Christian gloss to Twitchell's Hindu theology and practice, to make the group more appealing to the late 1980s. 'Regional eck spiritual aides' (Resas) became priests. A New Age temple was built, and called 'a church.' The meditation exercises were called 'prayer.' None of this had anything to do with any form of Christianity. It was pure marketing, out of the Twitchell playbook. It was another, corporate deception.

Sexual misconduct is another common characteristic of Eckankar leaders. Klemp and his predecessors have all been adulterers.

Twitchell previously married Camille Barlowe in Kentucky in the 1930s. Gross married Gail Twitchell, then younger Eckankar members, and had multiple relationships with senior initiates' wives including Bernadine Burlin.

Klemp married Margaret Burgon (known as 'Marjorie'), then Joan Tilton Cross, herself twice married before him.

Summarising all this, one gets quite a list: financial acquisition; multiple adultery; theft; deception. The list is inconsistent with spirituality, let alone 'mastership.'

The reality is Eckankar is just another pseudo-religious group or cult. And Klemp is just another leader of said group trying to obtain money by deceiving the membership. That followed Twitchell's unexpected death in Cincinnati in September 1971. So, Gail was the highest god? There is no evidence from her she consulted with the highest god.

Next, Harold Klemp. Klemp was appointed *by the Eckankar Board of Trustees* in 1981. The Board was then headed by Peter Skelskey after the Board deposed Darwin Gross. Doubtless Mr Skelskey will so confirm when he gives testimony in court on the point.

So much for the role of the imaginary Sugmad.

As a footnote, despite Twitchell's claims of an endless line of 'masters', Klemp has stated there will be no successor. The line ends with him.

Sugmad has apparently retired. Or he's on break. A long break.

More seriously, the test of a man's spirituality is of course his actual conduct. *By their fruit shall ye know them.* Twitchell was a pathological liar, driven by the desire to obtain money, not to foster religious education. What did Twitchell achieve? He achieved modest wealth for the Twitchell household, and prevented his wife Gail from leaving him as a result.

But, you ask, didn't Twitchell spread spiritual illumination, which would prove he was a Godman?

Good question. Very good.

Let's look at the evidence:

(1)   Twitchell committed adultery by marrying a second time. What God has joined together, no man can put asunder. When he slept with Gail, he was still joined spiritually and if you like karmically to Camille Barlowe. This kind of conduct offends the Holy Spirit.

(2)   Twitchell committed theft, in unacknowledged copyright thefts. See David Lane's thorough analysis of the thefts.

(3)   Twitchell failed to disclose his psychiatric history including arrest for attempted homicide in the Swami Premanda compound in Washington DC in the mid-1950s and detention in the St Elizabeth psychiatric hospital in DC.

(4)   Gross committed serial adultery after marrying Gail with other initiates' wives including Bernadine Burlin, and with numerous pretty girlfriends culled from the latest female entrants to the group.

(5)   Gross stole (Eckankar claimed) $2.5m in 1983 from corporate accounts.

(6)   Gross split with Eckankar, formed his own cult ATOM, and took a large part of the membership with him, thereby depriving the original cult of membership subscriptions and payments.

(7)   Eckankar has falsely claimed nonprofit status on the basis it is a religion for most of its existence, when it does not believe in god, its claims for contact with 'the eck' as a powerful spiritual force are empty and fraudulent, and its prayer or spiritual exercises are the vehicle for leaders to

practice magic tricks using thought control that keep the membership in a continuing state of delusion, nil personal growth, and spiritual failure.

(8)   Klemp is an adulterer, having left his wife Margaret Burgon and daughter Marion for his secretary, the serial adulterer Joan Cross who married Cross and Tilton before Klemp. That's a feast of sin right there.

(9)   Klemp is intolerant and unforgiving. The only initiate who claimed to have seen the Nine Silent Ones and experienced the 16th plane, the English initiate Mr Forsyth, was treated by Klemp as a dangerous dog. Klemp removed the initiations of him and his little group of disciples.

(10)   There is no body of spiritually advanced people in Eckankar.

(11)   Eckankar has not enhanced the spiritual life of anyone in any city in which it has taken space. Instead, it has imported demonic spirits and rampant materialism into every city it has gone into.

(12)   Eckankar violently attacks any non-compliant initiate or leaver. It's a living horror story.

So much for spiritual illumination being spread by Twitchell and Eckankar.

Score for big words: 100. Score for spiritual illumination: 0.

The group's claims to be a religion take it nowhere. It just is not a religion in any real sense, of worship of a God, a spiritual force, prayer. Serving Lucifer and his demons while claiming to worship Sugmad, which doesn't exist, is not belief in God. Using magic tricks to control initiates' minds is not belief in a spiritual force or prayer. These are false, fraudulent claims.

Eckankar does not even try hard to look like a religion. Klemp's quasi-Christian gloss on Twitchell's Hindu theology and practice was designed to make the group more appealing to the late 1980s.

'Regional eck spiritual aides' (Resas) became priests. A New Age temple was built in Chanhassen and called 'a church.' The tired meditation exercises were called 'prayer.'

None of this had anything to do with any form of Christianity. It was pure marketing, straight out of the Twitchell playbook. It was another, money-driven corporate deception.

Summarising all this, one gets quite a list: financial acquisition; multiple adultery; theft; deception. The list is inconsistent with spirituality, let alone 'mastership.' The so-called 'Masters' are full of passion, greed, sexual desire.

The reality is Eckankar is merely one of hundreds of pseudo-religious cults. Many of them, like Eckankar, grew up in the 1960s. Klemp is merely another cult leader obtaining pecuniary gain by deceiving the membership.

Conclusion

In the result, there is no Sugmad. It's marketing, folks.

If you want to find God, you won't find it in the Eckankar organisation, which is a derivative money hustle system. Sugmad is not God; it is a fabrication only. You need to study Radhasoami or Sant Mat or a similar Hindu tradition with a truly experienced Hindu teacher. You need to leave Eckankar and the big American sell behind and start again.

3

What is *'The Eck'*?

3.1   What is the Eck?

3.1.1 Introduction: the problem we need to face

What is the Eck that is so central to Eckankar? This chapter focuses on the Eck and what place it has (if any) in theology.

We start with the problem that the word does not mean what Eckists think it means. They believe it means 'the spirit of God', or the manifestation of the Sugmad. Unfortunately it doesn't.

Does this matter? Well, yes, unless you don't mind walking around talking like a fool.

3.1.2 The derivation of 'Eck'

In the previous chapter, at section 2.1, we explained the derivation of 'Eckankar' from the Sikh symbol meaning *'Ik Onkar'* or 'God is one.'

The key part of the Sikh phrase is not, however, 'Ik' but 'Onkar' or 'Oankar.' That is the part of the symbol that refers to supreme divinity: ੴ.

'Ik' is merely a *qualifier*, a pronoun meaning 'one.'

Twitchell, however, ever the superficial salesman, looking for a word that sounded different, preferred the 'Ik' part of the phrase as snappier. He rewrote it as 'Ek' or 'Eck' and designated it as meaning 'spirit of God.'

However, that is what 'Ik' does *not* mean. 'Ik' means 'one'; it is a word that qualifies 'God.' It describes an aspect of God. It is not equivalent to or the manifestation of God/Sugmad.

Now, when Eckists talk about 'the Eck' they mean 'the spirit of God' or 'the spirit that comes from the Sugmad.' They don't mean 'one.' But 'one' is what they are actually saying. When they proudly talk about being agents for the Eck (particularly self-important or pompous RESAs), they believe they mean they are agents for the Spirit of God.

Unfortunately not. What Eckists are actually saying is they are agents for 'one.' They have confused, like Twitchell before them, the 'Oankar' which is the supreme God, with the 'one' that qualifies it.

'Ik' or 'Eck' is no more than a pronoun meaning 'one' that qualifies the noun 'Oankar' or 'ankar'.

'Ik' or 'Eck' does *not* mean the spirit of God. It does *not* mean the expression of God, coming out of the Sugmad or God. It just means 'one', meaning, in Eckankar jargon, 'The Sugmad is one.'

'One' is not a manifestation of 'God', as the expression of God, but a subordinate qualification of God. That isin't really what Eckists want to say at all.

Eckists are talking to themselves (bad habit) or other Eckists about a pronoun, when they actually mean to refer to the noun. They're confused.

Just as the Sugmad is a made-up word, designed by founder Twitchell to distinguish his fledgling group from the many other groups marketing themselves as Hindu guru cults, with a differently named God that doesn't sound Hindu, so the Eck is a made up word.

Twitchell took the highly spiritual Sikh symbol, split it in two, and hit on the qualifier or pronoun part of the verbal expression of the symbol as the sellable bit.

This is marketing, folks, not spiritual education. It's not an answer to the question: What is God?

It's an answer to the question: *What sells?*

In the result, Twitchell prioritised marketing impact over sense. That illustrates yet again his primary business was selling, not spiritualising.

3.1.3 *The marketing of the eck*

What drove Twitchell's multiple copying and rewriting and polishing of other religious' theological concepts, and his endless copyright thefts, was what drives any modern marketing man: *find a new way to sell an old product.*

The test of any marketing campaign, newly coined jargon and stealing of the other guys' buzz phrases with a few changes is: *Does it sell?* The advice is always the same: *Get it right, and the money will flow.*

And, for a while, the money *did* flow. Twitchell's wholesale theft and mash-up of other religions, marketed with the commercial techniques he learned under Ron Hubbard at Scientology, chimed with the 1960s' fashion for New Age/Hindu movements.

The formula continued to work for a while after Twitchell died suddenly in September 1971. New Age religions were still popular in the corporatist 1970s. Twitchell was replaced in October 1971 by his widow Gail choosing her adulterous lover Darwin Gross as successor.

The group grew exponentially under his dynamic successor Darwin Gross.. Although semi-literate and poorly read, Gross injected personal charisma and energy into developing the group around the world.

By 1980, however, like every group, the cult had forgotten the magic that had led its early success and turned inward. In 1981 the Board of Eckankar swapped leaders, terminating the sexually overactive Gross who allegedly pocketed millions from the accounts, and appointing the safe, controllable, anonymous Harold Klemp.

That safe decision proved a bad one. No charisma, no commitment to growing the group, excessive shyness driving him to hide in his house. He spent his time writing, adding a layer of quasi-Christian terminology ('priests', 'church' etc) and substituting bedtime stories for theology.

It didn't sell. The formula was forgotten; the magic was lost. The group headed straight into the toilet, numbers in free fall. Currently the group, theoretically 'led' by Klemp who is now almost entirely a recluse, has been falling disastrously. Covid-19 is a further nail in its coffin. The party's over.

Which goes to show: *What sells today may not sell tomorrow.*

3.1.4 What is the Eck?

The Eck is *not* the spirit of God. Nor is it the oneness of God. It is a projection of occult power by a group of Tibetan demons called the Dharmapalas. See the discussion above, in section 2.2.

After the writer of this book escaped from Eckankar, he was given deliverance ministry, another word for exorcism (think *The Exorcist*).

The minister, a lifelong expert in deliverance (the practice of Jesus Christ's ministry of removing evil spirits from a person), told a conference later that day that *he had never seen so much evil on anyone.*

During their initiations every few years, Eckists believe they are getting a sound and perhaps a light or visual object for spiritual exercises in the next stage.

That is the surface experience. What is actually happening is *they are being infested with spirits.*

Because the Eckist puts himself or herself in the hands of the Eck and Klemp, coming into agreement with anything that Klemp/the Eck sends at them, they are vulnerable to infestation. And they get infested, initiation by initiation.

Klemp is the facilitator for the demonic powers of a group of extremely powerful and dangerous Tibetan demons led by Yama (see chapter 2). These demons, or Dharmapalas, control initiates by infesting them with spirits.

One of the spirits assigned to every Eckist is a small spirit (like a nasty Tinkerbell) who sits just above the top of your head. This is known as 'the demon of the top spot.' Other spirits relate to the weaknesses of the individuals, such as pride and vanity. Others infest the gastric system, living in the stomach area, or hang about the sexual parts.

The hard truth is that there is no 'Eck' spirit in Eckankar. There are only evil spirits possessed of a level of cunning and knowledge of human weakness that is vastly superior to the typical Eckist's grasp of psychic matters, let alone the workings of the spiritual worlds.

The Dharmapalas – the true name for the Nine Silent Ones, another marketing stunt – know you as you might know your Action Man or Barbie Doll toys, or your video game or movies, or your cars or your clothes. Eckists are easy prey for the Dharmapalas.

Conclusion: the Eck is a magic trick.

3.2   The Holy Spirit vs the eck

By contrast with the derivation of the Eck, a misconceived expression, and the Eck itself, the Holy Spirit enjoyed by Christians who have humbled themselves to God is all-powerful and glorious.

Who will take you to heaven: the Holy Spirit or the Eck? Easy. The Holy Spirit. Don't trust Eckankar. It's way too dangerous. fiction?

3.2.1 *The sound current of God?*

We now examine Eckankar's theological claim that 'the eck' is the sound current of God.

Which provokes some important questions. Is 'eck' the all-powerful force Eckankar claims? Or is it the Holy Spirit in

Christianity that is the true power? Or is this just an argument about words?

The answer: it is the Holy Spirit of Jesus Christ and Christianity that is the true spiritual force.

This is not an argument about names. 'Eck' is not a spiritual force at all. It is a demonic power directed by Tibetan evil spirits.

The 'sound current' in various noises, copied from Shabda Yoga, is substituted in Eckankar for a set of small demons attached to the initiate in the initiation ritual.

For example, the writer recalls a small demon leaving his head during his deliverance (exorcism). As this small demon left, the 'sound current' cut off.

It was irrefutable evidence. The 'sound current' of 'eck' is a demon of hell.

The word 'Eck', let's remember, is just a misconceived fabrication, copied but misunderstood from Hindu religion (see section 2.1).

3.2.2 *The Holy Spirit heals, the eck does nothing*

By contrast, the Holy Spirit is the true power of the true God, Yah Weh. It can change illness into health and restore a missing body part, or raise a corpse back to life.

'Eck' can't do any of these things. 'Eck' is a useless demon.

There are so many examples of the action of the living power of God cf.'the eck.' The Holy Spirit heals bodies. Jesus commanded the dead to rise, and they rose. In Eckankar, if someone has a problem, the normal response is, *don't get involved, it's just their karma.*

Seriously? Eckists don't care about others because that's *their* karma. They're dysfunctional. God is infinite love and care.

3.2.3 *The violence of eck*

In reality, 'the eck' cannot and will not help you. That is because it is a destructive carrier of a devouring and malicious evil power originating in Tibet.

To the compliant initiate, the Eckankar life is harmony and growth, because you see and feel it with blind eyes. To the non compliant, to those it targets, these members are being tricked by a violent power directed by Tibetan spirits and magiciians.

But let's take some examples. Judge for yourself.

In *Child in the Wilderness*, Klemp relates how he brought in a violent power into the workplace that disturbed the other workers. This story is funny and acceptable only to Eckists, who don't care about other people.

In other incidents in *Child in the Wilderness*, Klemp describes feeling compelled to take off his clothes in the departure lounge of Milwaukee International Airport.

By the way, don't believe Klemp's cleaned up version. He didn't stop at his shirt, people. If he had he wouldn't have been arrested! Of course, he undressed to naked. That was why he was arrested, convicted and sentenced to the County Hospital in Milwaukee for psychiatric treatment.

Then there's Klemp's belief he is in touch with God, so much so he has to jump off a bridge in Milwaukee in midwinter into a freezing river.

These are examples of the impact of the violent force that is eck on the member. By 'violent force', we mean 'demonic power.' In traditional terms, it's the power of the Devil.

Eck has essentially violent. It has two faces: soft, snakelike but compelling, and viciously aggressive/destructive. These are, of course, the key characteristics of Twitchell and Klemp. The magicians including the self-described 'masters' are the servants of this power.

Klemp is a weak carrier of this power, but Gross was much more powerful. Ever see Gross walk? You could see the power around him, the height and width of a Greek temple column. Gross could be soft and charming, and play harmonious vibes, but his anger was absolute. It is the nature of this power that it controls its carrier and expresses itself through him.

All so true, so occult. But why do we say *violent*, you ask?

The eck attacks and tries to displace and drive out the Holy Spirit. This is the action of evil on what is good, Lucifer, Twitchell's true Master, hates God for throwing him out of heaven. The eck tries to destroy the presence of God wherever possible. 'Eck' is above all a devouring spirit.

Contrast the Holy Spirit, the infinitely kind breath of God. The Holy Spirit is gentle yet all-powerful. With extraordinary speed it can open a man's mind in a fraction of a second to new knowledge, specific and relevant. And the Holy Spirit is never, ever violent.

FOLLOW THE HOLY SPIRIT
AND SEE YOUR LIFE CHANGE